D1717019

NATURE'S GROSSEST

WHALE POOP

By Bert Wilberforce

Gareth Stevens
PUBLISHING

Please visit our website, www.garethstevens.com. For a free color catalog of all our high-quality books, call toll free 1-800-542-2595 or fax 1-877-542-2596.

Library of Congress Cataloging-in-Publication Data

Wilberforce, Bert, author.
  Whale poop / Bert Wilberforce.
      pages cm. — (Nature's grossest)
  Includes bibliographical references and index.
  ISBN 978-1-4824-1863-7 (pbk.)
  ISBN 978-1-4824-1861-3 (6 pack)
  ISBN 978-1-4824-1862-0 (library binding)
  1. Whales—Physiology—Juvenile literature. 2. Animal droppings—Juvenile literature. 3. Ambergris—Juvenile literature. I. Title.
  QL737.C4W4914 2015
  599.5—dc23
                                    2014031945

Published in 2015 by
Gareth Stevens Publishing
111 East 14th Street, Suite 349
New York, NY 10003

Copyright © 2015 Gareth Stevens Publishing

Designer: Katelyn E. Reynolds
Editor: Therese Shea

Photo credits: Cover, pp. 1, 15 Reinhard Dirscherl/WaterFrame/Getty Images; pp. 3–24 (background) Oleksii Natykach/Shutterstock.com; p. 5 Alexey Mhoyan/Shutterstock.com; p. 7 (beluga whale) fotofactory/Shutterstock.com; p. 7 (humpback whale) Jordan Tan/ Shutterstock.com; p. 9 Lledo/Shutterstock.com; p. 11 Mogens Trolle/Shutterstock.com; p. 13 Robert King/Newsmakers/Getty Images; p. 17 alybaba/Shutterstock.com; p. 19 Peter Kaminski/Wikipedia.com; p. 21 Ethan Daniels/Shutterstock.com.

Printed in the United States of America

CPSIA compliance information: Batch #CW15GS: For further information contact Gareth Stevens, New York, New York at 1-800-542-2595.

CONTENTS

Wonderful Whales 4

Protected by Poop! 12

Floating Gold 16

Not Just Whale Waste 20

Glossary 22

For More Information 23

Index 24

Boldface words appear in the glossary.

Wonderful Whales

Whales live in waters all over the world. The blue whale is the largest animal ever! It can be as long as 100 feet (30 m)! Many other species, or kinds, of whales are much smaller. There are about 80 species of whales.

Some whales have teeth, such as sperm whales and beluga whales. They eat fish and **squid**. Some whales have **baleen**. Baleen lets water out of a whale's mouth, but traps tiny sea animals the whale eats. Humpback whales and blue whales have baleen.

beluga whale

teeth

humpback whale

baleen

Different kinds of whales have different **behaviors**. Some toothed whales travel in groups called pods. They can "talk" to each other. They can also use sound to find, or locate, objects in water. This is called echolocation.

Baleen whales usually like to be alone. However, some kinds of baleen whales travel together thousands of miles each year to have babies in warm waters. Then they travel back to colder waters where there's more food.

Protected by Poop!

Dwarf sperm whales and pygmy sperm whales are toothed whales. They're less than 12 feet (3.7 m) long. They're also not very fearsome. So, these small whales face danger from predators such as sharks. However, they have a secret **weapon**—poop!

Dwarf and pygmy sperm whales can **release** a cloud of waste into the water. They can hide in the cloud until danger has passed! If they swim away and a predator chases them, they can continue to release poop clouds behind them.

15

Floating Gold

A special kind of sperm whale poop is called ambergris (AM-buhr-grihs). It's made of a matter that helps whales eat tough things like squid **beaks**. After the waste is released, it hardens over many years in the ocean and in the sun.

Ambergris is valuable because it's used to make **perfume**. An 8-year-old boy found a piece on a beach in New Zealand. It was only 1.3 pounds (0.6 kg), but it was worth $65,000! That's why some people call ambergris "floating gold."

19

Not Just Whale Waste

Scientists say whale poop of all kinds is an important part of keeping ocean waters healthy. Whale waste carries **nutrients** to different parts of the ocean. Plants and animals need these to live. Who knew poop could be so helpful? Now you do!

GLOSSARY

baleen: the thin, flat, tough growths hanging from the upper jaw of some whales that are used to separate food from water

beak: a part of the mouth that sticks out on some animals and is used to tear food

behavior: the way an animal acts

nutrient: something a living thing needs to grow and stay alive

perfume: a liquid that is placed on the skin to give off a pleasant smell

release: to let go

squid: a sea creature that has eight arms, two tentacles, two fins, and a long body

weapon: something used to fight an enemy

FOR MORE INFORMATION

BOOKS

Petrie, Kristin. *Dwarf Sperm Whales*. Edina, MN: ABDO Publishing, 2006.

Rodríguez, Ana María. *Secret of the Sleepless Whales—and More!* Berkeley Heights, NJ: Enslow Publishers, 2009.

Turnbull, Steph. *Whale*. Mankato, MN: Smart Apple Media, 2013.

WEBSITES

Whale
www.worldwildlife.org/species/whale
Read about many kinds of whales.

Whales
www.defenders.org/whales/basic-facts
Find out why whales in the wild are in trouble and how people are helping them.

INDEX

ambergris 16, 18

baleen 6, 10

beluga whales 6

blue whale 4, 6

dwarf sperm whales
    12, 14

echolocation 8

humpback whales 6

nutrients 20

perfume 18

pods 8

predators 12, 14

pygmy sperm whales
    12, 14

species 4

sperm whales 6, 16

teeth 6, 8, 12

waste clouds 14

DATE DUE

			PRINTED IN U.S.A.